D1709483

HOW YOUR BODY WORKS

FIGHTING ILLNESS AND INJURY

THE IMMUNE SYSTEM

THOMAS CANAVAN

PowerKiDS press

Published in 2016 by
The Rosen Publishing Group, Inc.
29 East 21ˢᵗ Street, New York, NY 10010

Cataloging-in-Publication Data
Canavan, Thomas.
Fighting illness and injury: the immune system / by Thomas Canavan.
p. cm. — (How your body works)
Includes index.
ISBN 978-1-4994-1223-9 (pbk.)
ISBN 978-1-4994-1247-5 (6 pack)
ISBN 978-1-4994-1233-8 (library binding)
1. Immune system — Juvenile literature. I. Canavan, Thomas, 1956-.
II. Title.
QR181.8 C218 2016
616.07'9—d23

Copyright © 2016 Arcturus Holding Limited

Produced by Arcturus Publishing Limited,

Author: Thomas Canavan
Editors: Joe Harris, Joe Fullman, Nicola Barber and Sam Williams
Designer: Elaine Wilkinson
Original design concept and cover design: Notion Design

Picture Credits: All images courtesy of Shutterstock, apart from: Lee
Montgomery and Anne Sharp: back cover, p30, p31. Science Photo Library:
p3 bottom, p6 middle-left (Biophoto Associates).

All rights reserved. No part of this book may be reproduced in any form
without permission in writing from the publisher, except by a reviewer.

Manufactured in the United States of America
CPSIA Compliance Information: Batch #WS15PK:
For Further Information contact Rosen Publishing, New York, New York at 1-800-237-9932

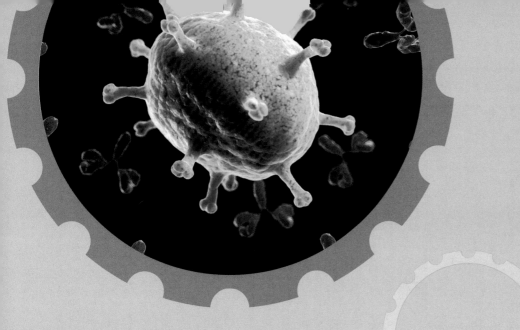
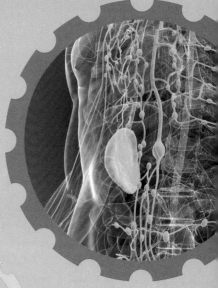

CONTENTS

AUG 2 2 2016

DEFENSIVE ACTION

Your body is amazing! It is always on guard, ready to fight off attacks by germs that could make you ill. Although you're surrounded by millions of these germs each day, your body sets up barriers to deal with most of them before they can harm you.

Even if nasty germs make it past your defensive barriers, your body has lots of weapons to do battle. Those weapons are part of your immune system. They fight to isolate and get rid of nasty invaders. Once they succeed, they remember how they won, so it will be easier to fight off that type of attack next time.

Your defensive systems remain active even after they've dealt with an infection or injury. It's just as important to make sure you can heal and recover fully. Leaving that job half done would make you an easy target for more problems.

INVISIBLE ENEMIES

Most of the germs that make you unwell are either bacteria, fungi, protozoa, or viruses.

Bacteria are tiny one-celled creatures – they are everywhere around you and even inside you! Most bacteria won't hurt you, and many do useful jobs such as helping with digestion. But some bacteria are harmful and can make you ill.

Protozoa are also one-celled creatures. Most protozoa are harmless, but some cause serious diseases such as malaria and dysentery.

Fungi are tiny relatives of mushrooms that live in damp places. Athlete's foot is a fungal infection that you can catch if you don't dry your feet properly.

Viruses live inside the cells of plants or animals. Once inside a cell they take over the cell to reproduce. In humans, viruses cause illnesses such as colds, chickenpox, and flu.

GERM WARFARE

Germs are tiny, harmful living organisms. There are several different types, and they're all so small you cannot see them with the naked eye. That's why you have to be extra careful to protect yourself from them. Your body will defend itself if these germs get inside you, but you can help keep your body healthy by taking steps to stop them in their tracks.

A GOOD CLEAN

Your skin is your first line of protection against most types of infection. But it's important to keep it clean. Washing your hands thoroughly helps prevent the spread of colds, flu, food poisoning, and many other illnesses. A good tip is to sing "Happy Birthday to You" twice while you wash. Then you'll have done a good job!

WAITING TO ATTACK

You can pick up germs almost anywhere! They could be in the food you eat, on dirty door handles or computer keyboards. Germs can even be in the air you breathe if someone has spread germs by coughing or sneezing. When you eat, germs from your hands can go in your mouth. Or rubbing your eyes with a dirty finger spreads the germs in your eyes. Luckily, your body has lots of ways of defending you from germ attack.

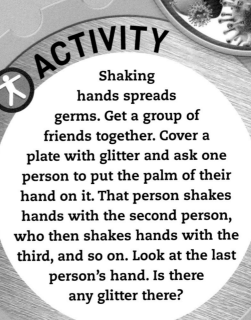

The name malaria comes from Italian words meaning "bad air," which is what people once thought caused the disease!

⊕ ACTIVITY

Shaking hands spreads germs. Get a group of friends together. Cover a plate with glitter and ask one person to put the palm of their hand on it. That person shakes hands with the second person, who then shakes hands with the third, and so on. Look at the last person's hand. Is there any glitter there?

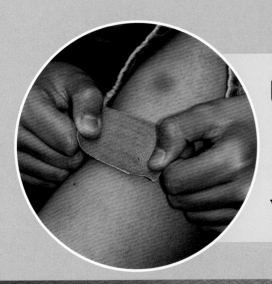

DO NOT PASS "GO"

One of the most common ways for germs to attack is through wounds, like cuts or scrapes. If your protective layer of skin is removed, then germs find it easier to enter your body. That's why it is important to dab a cut with antiseptic to clean it, and to cover it while it heals.

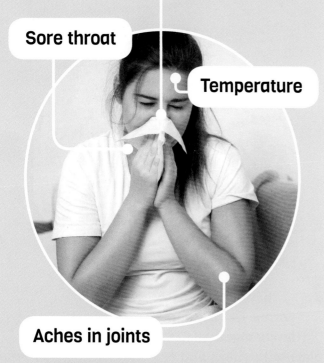

Runny nose

Sore throat

Temperature

Aches in joints

RAPID RESPONSE

Even with your skin protecting you, and your own good work to stay clean, germs can enter your body. That's when your immune system starts to fight back. It gets rid of some germs almost as soon as they arrive. And if germs do get past and start to make you ill, your body does its best to limit the damage.

SUFFERING THE SYMPTOMS

When you catch a cold or develop the flu, you begin to feel uncomfortable in various ways. Your nose becomes stuffed up or runny. You may have a headache or a high temperature, and your joints may begin to ache. These symptoms are usually signs that your immune system is acting to get rid of the virus. Aching joints are painful evidence of infection, but they might also be your body's way of telling you not to move around too much. That way, your body can concentrate more on fighting the infection and less on providing energy for your muscles.

MIGHTY MUCUS

Your nose is always making gooey mucus, even when you're well. Mucus stops the skin inside your nose from drying out, and it stops lots of germs from going any further into your body and making you ill. If you have a cold, your nose works even harder to fight off the infection. The mucus gets thicker and stickier. That's why you go through all of those tissues when you catch a cold!

Area where mucus is produced

AH-CHOO!

Did you know that a sneeze travels at 100 miles per hour (160 km/h)! A sneeze is your body's way of getting rid of an irritating – or attacking – object out of your nose and mouth. Signals pass along the nerves to tell the muscles in your diaphragm, stomach, chest, and throat to work together to make that sudden blast of air. A single sneeze can get rid of 100,000 germs!

A 12-year-old girl named Donna Griffiths had a sneezing fit that lasted 978 days. It's estimated that she sneezed a million times during that period!

IT MUST BE SOMETHING I ATE!

Germs sometimes catch a ride into your body on something you eat or drink. Your body recognizes the invaders and tries to get rid of them as fast as possible. The fastest way is often vomiting or throwing up. You may feel a bit unwell after vomiting because it's such a violent act. But you will probably soon begin to feel a little better!

FIGHTING BACK

Although your body does a good job of defending itself from germ invaders – or sending them off promptly – germs do sometimes settle in for a battle. Your immune system then has to destroy these invisible invaders. It will also remember how it did the job, so that next time you'll be protected.

Scabs start to form less than ten seconds after you cut yourself!

CODE RED!

Your blood contains cells to combat infection. Imagine that you fall and cut yourself, and the cut gets infected. On the surface, cells called platelets form a scab to stop other germs from getting in. Inside, white blood cells use special chemicals to digest foreign germs. Once they've used up all of their chemicals they die, along with the attacking germs.

BLOOD, SPIT, AND TEARS

The battle for your body is fought on many different fronts, and you don't have to be cut and bleeding to risk infection. Your body can tell whether a certain type of bacteria in your mouth belongs there to help you digest – or if it's an intruder. Your saliva contains chemicals that can destroy the outer walls of invading bacteria and viruses. Your tears also contain antibodies and can destroy germs if they get into your eyes.

SEEK AND DESTROY

Your blood contains proteins called antibodies that identify and destroy harmful germs. They are shown attacking a virus in the image on the right. Antibodies can tell the difference between dangerous germs, and the helpful bacteria that your body needs. Antibodies attach themselves to the attackers and either destroy them, or send them along to special cells that digest the attackers.

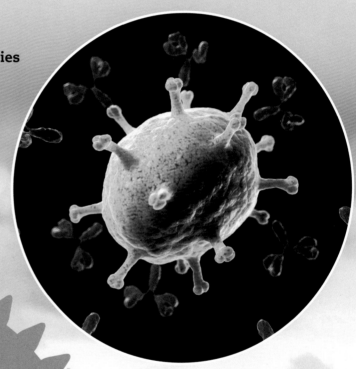

ANTIBODIES NEVER FORGET!

As it fights infection, your body uses a type of "memory" to prepare for future conflict. Once antibodies have done their job, they help other cells remember how the attackers were identified and destroyed. So the next time that type of germ attacks, your body is able to respond more quickly. That's why if you've had certain diseases, such as chickenpox or mumps, you rarely catch them again.

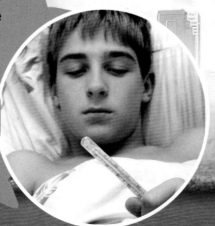

LYMPHATIC SYSTEM

Blood isn't the only fluid running through your body. The lymphatic system is often called your body's "drainage network." But the liquid flowing slowly through it – lymph – also contains cells that work hard to defend you against infection.

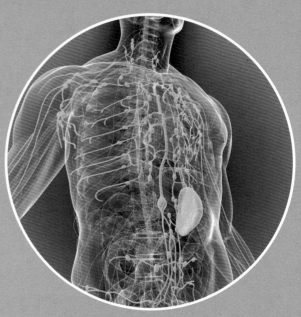

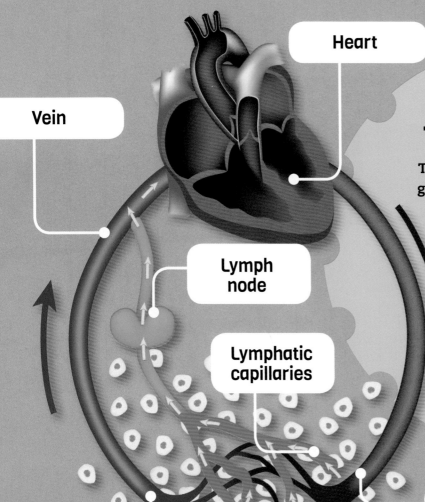

Heart

Vein

Lymph node

Lymphatic capillaries

Blood capillaries

Artery

Tissue cells

PRECIOUS TRANSPORT

The lymphatic system (shown in green on the left and above) extends across your whole body. It helps to keep your body's fluids in balance by absorbing some of the extra liquid that builds up between tissue cells and returning it to your veins. Upon entering the system, it becomes part of another liquid – lymph – which also contains wastes that need to be filtered out.

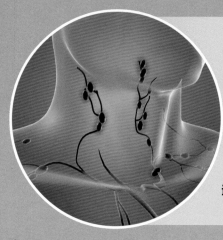

SWOLLEN GLANDS

You sometimes hear a person say "I'm not well – my glands are swollen." They're probably talking about the lymph nodes (which some people call glands) on the sides of their neck or under their arms. These nodes swell up when their white blood cells are battling infection. The swelling isn't an illness in itself – it's actually a sign that the body is fighting an infection.

KILLER CELLS

Different white blood cells wage war against invaders. B cells become active when an attacker has been identified. Then they produce the antibodies to fight them. T cells sometimes battle your body's own cells – if they've been altered by infection. NK (Natural Killer) cells are even more powerful than T cells.

NK cells check the protein on every cell they meet, and poison those with an unfamiliar coating!

Cervical lymph nodes (in the face and neck)

Thoracic duct (collects the lymph from around the body)

Axillary nodes (in the armpits)

FIGHTING INFECTION

The lymphatic network has another important job which connects it to your immune system. Lymph moves slowly because it's not pumped the way blood is. Your muscles squeeze it along, and it passes through small masses of tissue, called lymph nodes, along the way. These nodes contain white blood cells that identify harmful germs and destroy them. Other white blood cells produce the antibodies that scout for invaders.

Cisterna chyli (lymph reservoir; filters out fat from the intestines)

Spleen (like a large lymph node – contains white blood cells that fight infection)

Inguinal lymph nodes (in the legs and groin)

TEMPERATURE CONTROL

Your body needs to stay at a steady temperature in order to remain healthy. It's just like a car that runs poorly in the cold or overheats in hot weather. Luckily it has many ways of adjusting its temperature. It even uses that ability to keep you healthy.

HOT AND COLD

You know if you're feeling too hot or too cold. Nerves send signals to your brain to warn you. The warning is important because your body needs to stay at around 98.6°F (37°C) to work at its best. An area of your brain called the hypothalamus is very sensitive to any temperature change. It springs into action to get your body back to that ideal temperature.

WHEN IT'S COLD...

- Blood vessels near your skin's cold surface tighten, so that not much warm blood passes through them. This may make you look a bit pale!
- Tiny hairs on your skin stand up away from your skin, to try and trap some warm air around your skin.

Shivering uses energy stored in fat to power the muscles as they twitch!

SHIVER ME TIMBERS

One of the best ways your body uses to warm up is shivering. Your brain sends messages to your muscles, getting them to twitch. That twitching, or shivering, releases heat. Your jaw might even start shivering, causing your teeth to chatter.

THE IDEAL RANGE

There's a good reason why your body needs to keep itself close to its ideal temperature. Every moment your body is carrying out millions of chemical reactions – to release energy, to send messages, to digest food. And those chemical reactions depend on proteins called enzymes to work properly. Enzymes begin to lose their strength if the temperature gets too hot or too cold. Once that happens, your body's systems stop working so well.

NO SWEAT!

The best way to cool down is to sweat. As sweat is mostly water, it rises or evaporates when it comes into contact with air. The water molecules go from being liquid to being a gas, and mixing with the air. They take some of their heat with them as they leave your body. You often sweat during a fever, to make sure that your body doesn't get too hot.

FEVERISH ACTIVITY

Sometimes your temperature goes up when you're fighting an infection. If it rises above 100.4°F (38°C), you probably have a fever. In your brain, the hypothalamus receives information that your body is fighting an infection. It sends out information to keep heat trapped inside, so that your temperature rises. That raised temperature, called a fever, is hot enough to help fight germs (and even destroy some of them). But it's not hot enough to damage the enzymes in your body.

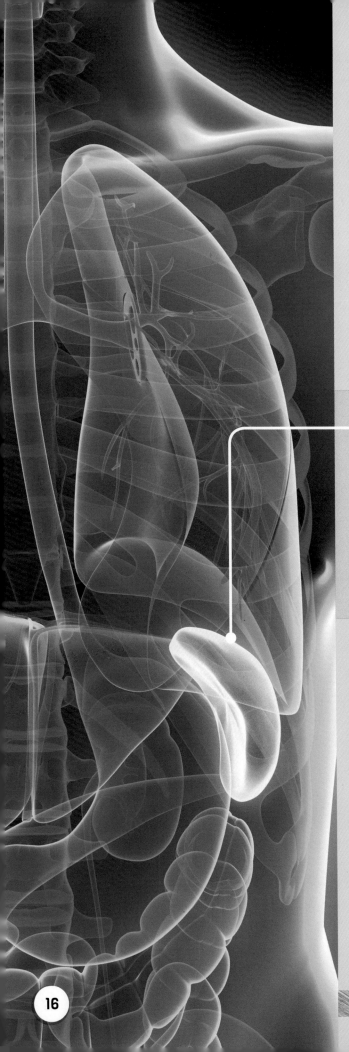

SUPER ORGANS

As well as their main jobs, many of your body's organs have other tasks to do. Your spleen, for example, is an efficient blood filter but it also teams up with the lymphatic system to do some germ-hunting. And it's not the only organ doing double – or triple – duty.

FILTER AND FIGHTER

Your spleen is an organ about the size of an adult's hand. It is tucked in the upper left of your abdomen behind your stomach. Its main job is to filter red blood cells, getting rid of those that no longer work properly and recycling the valuable iron that they contain. But your immune system also depends on the work of your spleen.

BLOOD DEFENDER

The spleen is also part of the lymphatic system. Being such an important junction for blood and lymph has real advantages. Special white blood cells called macrophages surround the dead cells that have been filtered out of the blood and carry them away. They act in the same way with germ invaders. If nasty bacteria or viruses float in, the spleen produces "defender" white bloods cell called lymphocytes. They're the cells that produce the antibodies to fight attacking germs.

TEARS: TWICE AS USEFUL

Your tears do more than just rinse your eyes out. They contain a powerful enzyme called lysozyme, which attacks invading bacteria. It eats into the outer wall of bacteria, destroying them so that they can be washed away. You also find lysozyme doing the same job in your saliva, mucus, and even in the milk that nursing babies drink.

Bile produced by the spleen is bitter-tasting. The ancient Greeks linked the spleen to bitter, or angry, moods in people!

MEGA LIVER

Your liver carries out over 500 jobs. Most of the jobs involve making and storing fuel from the food you eat, cleaning your blood, or helping you digest fats. But it also helps you recover from illness. The liver takes out the important ingredients from the medicines you take. Then, it sends them to where they're needed. It also helps to stop bleeding by causing your blood to thicken, or clot.

BRILLIANT BONES

The spongy central section of your bones, called the marrow, is a blood-cell factory. It's known mainly for producing the red blood cells that transport oxygen and nutrients throughout your body. But it also makes white blood cells and platelets that are two vital parts of your immune system.

TEAMWORK

If you find yourself in a dangerous situation with a group of other people, the smart thing to do is work together. It's the same for your body's organs and systems. They all work together as a team to keep your body running smoothly. If one part isn't working as well as it should, the others come to its aid.

PARTNERS

Your immune system needs other systems to work well. One of its most important partners is the system which triggers hormones. Some of these hormones decide how sensitive your immune system is or how hard it should be working. Hormones instruct different parts of your body by delivering chemical signals. Your body's cells and tissues respond to these chemical changes. These chemical reactions produce physical changes – blood vessels might tighten or widen, muscles might begin to twitch, or more cells might be created to form a scab over a cut.

Sweat glands in your feet produce around 17.5 fluid ounces (500ml) of sweat each day!

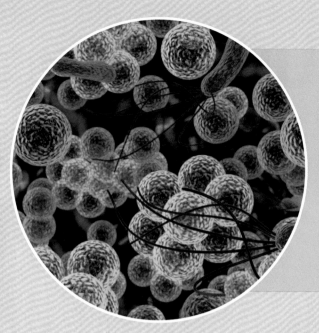

GOOD BACTERIA

Some of your body's fiercest defenders are actually bacteria. In fact, these "good bacteria" outnumber the harmful bacteria in many parts of your body. Many of them live in your intestines, ready to destroy harmful invaders. Other helpful bacteria alert the rest of your immune system to invasions.

HELPING EACH OTHER

Organs and systems team up to support each other if they are damaged or weakened. Although your spleen plays an important role in your immune system, you can survive without it – other organs and systems just have to work a little harder. Your liver takes over the filtering of your blood and your lymphatic system produces more white cells to attack invading germs.

READY TO EAT

Imagine seeing and smelling some delicious pastries. Your eyes send information about what to expect, and your nose sends signals about how good it will taste. All that information travels to your brain, which tells your mouth to water. The saliva is important for digesting the food. But your saliva also contains lysozyme, an enzyme that destroys any harmful bacteria that may arrive with your food. So you're not just ready for a real treat – your body is guarding you against attack.

COLD SWEAT

Sweat also plays a role as part of your defensive team. It can be triggered by your nervous system. The brain recognizes a stressful situation and tells the adrenal gland to release epinephrine, which makes you sweat. Why is this? Sweat is slippery, so it might make it hard for a predator to keep hold of you. Sweat also has antibacterial properties, to help protect you from germs.

INJURY TIME

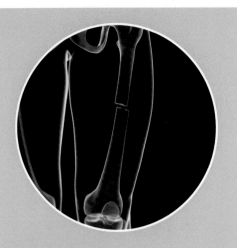

If you've ever fallen and broken your arm, sprained an ankle while running, or even had a painful paper cut, you'll know that the injury hasn't lasted forever. Your body has ways of repairing itself and helping you recover from injuries.

STICKS AND STONES...

Your bones may be strong and flexible but they can still break, especially if they are forced too hard. They're a bit like wooden pencils, or twigs, which will bend and bend until . . . they snap! A snap, or broken bone, is called a fracture. The first thing you'll feel if you've broken a bone is a lot of pain. It hurts so much you probably won't even try to use that arm or leg, or you risk making things even worse.

REPAIR WORK

When you break a bone, blood cells form a clot around the break. Special cells clean away floating bits of bone and kill any germs in the area. Over the next two weeks, a soft-tissue covering builds up over the fracture. Different cells, called osteoblasts, make more bone to make a hard covering. Other cells, called osteoclasts, then clear away any extra bone that has formed around the fracture. This continues until the bone is back to its original shape.

X MARKS THE SPOT

Doctors can take pictures of your bones to check whether you've had a fracture. X-rays are a type of radiation that pass through your body. The x-rays are absorbed at different rates by soft parts, like skin or muscle, and harder substances such as bones. In the x-ray picture, bones show up clearly as white shapes, just like a light shining through fog will pick out the shape of a person or car.

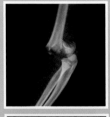
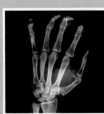

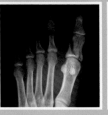
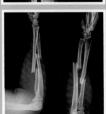
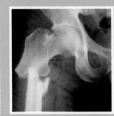

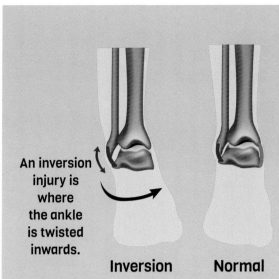

An inversion injury is where the ankle is twisted inwards.

Inversion

Normal

Eversion

An eversion injury is where the ankle is twisted outwards.

WHAT A STRAIN!

You can hurt your muscles and ligaments as well as your bones. If you stretch a muscle too much, you can strain it. Muscle strains are most common in the neck and back. If ligaments get stretched too far, the injury is called a sprain. A severe sprain is when the ligaments are torn. It's quite easy to sprain an ankle if you step on something uneven and your ankle turns suddenly.

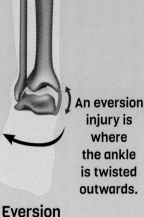

BUMPS AND BRUISES

If you bump yourself, you may get a black or purple bruise. This forms when the injury breaks tiny blood vessels, and they leak into the tissue nearby. One of these bruises on your cheek can give you a black eye.

SOLAR BURNING

Radiation in sunlight is good for your body, but only in small doses. After that, it starts to destroy the living cells in the outer layer of your skin. This can lead to painful sunburn. Your immune system responds by opening up blood vessels to send in healing white blood cells. This increased blood flow makes your skin feel warmer and look redder. To reduce the chance of sunburn, always use sunscreen, which blocks out much of the harmful radiation from the sun.

OUTSIDE HELP

Your body is amazing at fighting disease and healing itself when it's injured. But there are times when it needs a boost to get the job done. Doctors, nurses, and other medical professionals have tools and techniques to make you better – or to stop you from getting ill in the first place. After all, prevention is better than cure.

A SHOT IN THE ARM

As a baby, you would probably have been vaccinated against a number of diseases, but you were too young to remember. Vaccination is usually a fairly painless injection. It uses your body's own antibodies to stop you from catching serious diseases. A vaccination contains a mild version of that disease. It's too weak to make you feel very bad, but strong enough to get your body defending against it.

One of the best things about the way antibodies fight diseases is the "memories" they leave behind (see page 11). These are chemical records of the disease they fought, and how they got rid of it. If you're exposed to that same disease again – even in its strong version – your body can call on that information to make it harmless.

BONE PROTECTION

Although your body is able to heal a broken bone, the whole process takes time. The two bits of bone need to be lined up properly to make sure the healed bone grows back straight. Once the bone is in the right place, you'll probably have a cast put over it. That's a hard covering to keep the bone protected and stop it from being bumped out of place.

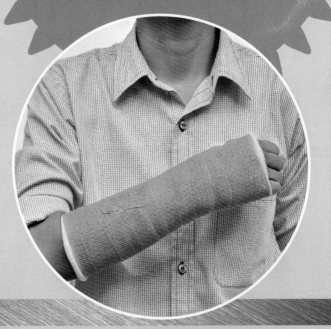

A STITCH IN TIME

If you've had a deep cut, you might need to get stitched up. Sewing the sections of skin on either side of a cut back together stops the bleeding, helps keep out germs and lets your body start healing. Most modern stitches just dissolve once they've done their job.

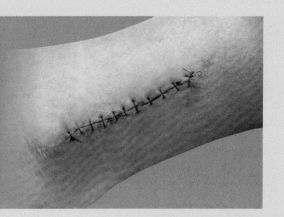

WALK OF LIFE

In the past, if people were born without limbs or lost them to injury, they would have to manage without, or use very basic, wooden replacements. Modern technology has revolutionized limb replacements, or prostheses. It has given many people the chance to type, hold a pen, stand, run, and ski. Some modern artificial limbs are even mind-controlled, so they can obey a person's thoughts.

Over 200 years ago, cowpox, a weak cousin of the deadly disease smallpox, was used for the first vaccinations. Some people feared that patients might actually turn into cows!

ACTIVITY

See whether you can make an artificial hand that can pick something up. Use a pair of cooking tongs to see how effective they are. Try picking up different objects – maybe a tennis ball, a pebble, and a coin. Can you think of ways to make your "hand" work better, maybe by attaching something to it?

DID YOU KNOW?

YOUR TEARS HAVE DIFFERENT SHAPES, DEPENDING ON WHY THEY ARE BEING PRODUCED

You produce three main types of tear – one when you're really happy or sad, one to keep your eye moist, and one to clean the eye when dust or other objects get in it. When magnified thousands of times under a powerful microscope, these tears look very different – mainly because of the chemicals that make them up.

HEALERS WERE PROBABLY PERFORMING BRAIN SURGERY AS LONG AS 5,000 YEARS AGO

Ancient human skulls found near Stonehenge in the UK have revealed carefully carved holes in the bone. Archaeologists believe that these holes were made with stone tools by healers. The holes probably relieved pressure on the brain resulting from a head wound.

THERE'S A GOOD REASON WHY ANIMALS LICK THEIR WOUNDS AND HUMANS KISS THEIR CHILDREN'S BUMPS AND BRUISES

It's all because of saliva, which contains powerful chemicals to fight off infection from bacteria. Saliva also contains substances that help nerves and skin to grow back. That's why wounds that take weeks to heal on your skin will often heal within a few days inside your mouth.

SOME LIFESAVING MEDICINES ARE MADE FROM POISONOUS INGREDIENTS

One example helps people who have been bitten by poisonous snakes. To make the medicine, scientists obtain some of the poisonous venom by "milking" a snake. They then inject a horse or other large animal with a small amount of the venom – not enough to harm the animal. The horse produces antibodies called antivenom to fight off the attack. Scientists can then extract some of this antivenom from the horse's blood – and use it to make medicines to treat snake bites in humans.

EVEN MINOR SUNBURNS CAN CAUSE LASTING DAMAGE

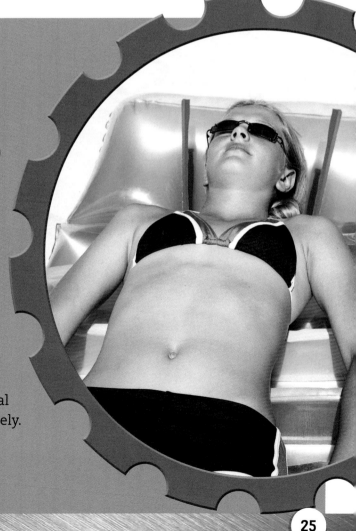

Scientists have examined people with minor cases of sunburn in the months afterwards. They have observed that blood vessels damaged in the original sunburn can take up to 15 months to heal completely.

FREQUENTLY ASKED QUESTIONS

WHY DOES BEING COLD GIVE YOU A COLD?

Scientists often dismiss the connection between "getting cold" and "getting a cold." That's because the common cold is caused by a virus, which can spread in just about any temperature. But some scientists have added a new twist. In experiments, people exposed to cold and damp really did develop symptoms of a cold. Why? One theory is that cold temperatures cause blood vessels in the nose and throat to narrow, meaning they are less able to deliver infection-fighting white blood cells to combat the cold virus.

IS IT HARMFUL TO SWALLOW YOUR OWN PHLEGM?

You swallow enough phlegm to fill five cans of cola each day – so hopefully it's not harmful! Phlegm is the mucus that is produced in your respiratory passages to capture dust and other damaging particles. Hairlike cells called cilia line those passages and "brush" the phlegm up to your throat. Although phlegm looks and feels slimy, it doesn't cause problems once you swallow it. Powerful enzymes and acids in your digestive system break it down to make it harmless.

WHY DO SCABS ITCH SO MUCH?

Scabs are shields that protect healing skin from infection. Doctors have several theories why scabs itch. One is that they contain histamines, chemicals that slightly irritate the skin near the wound. Scratching this itch removes the scab once it has done its job. Another theory is that scabs begin to pull away as the skin heals, causing an itchy feeling.

WHAT CAUSES BLISTERS?

A blister is a small pocket of fluid that forms on the upper layer of your skin. The fluid, called serum, is the clear liquid of your blood once the red blood cells and other materials have been removed. You can develop a blister after being exposed to heat or chemicals, but usually the cause is friction – shoes that rub your feet, for example. The fluid acts as a cushion, letting the tissue below heal. That's why you should never pop a blister.

SYSTEMS OF THE BODY

Skeletal system

The skeletal system supports and protects your body.

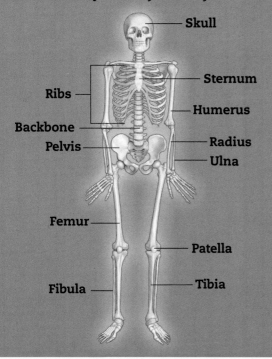

- Skull
- Sternum
- Ribs
- Humerus
- Backbone
- Radius
- Pelvis
- Ulna
- Femur
- Patella
- Fibula
- Tibia

Muscular system

The muscular system moves your body.

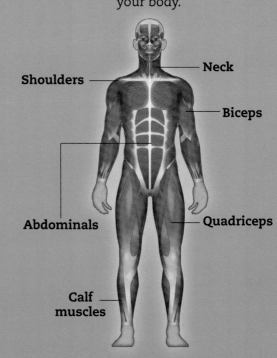

- Neck
- Shoulders
- Biceps
- Abdominals
- Quadriceps
- Calf muscles

Circulatory system

The circulatory system moves blood around your body.

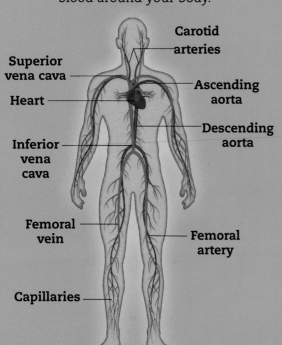

- Carotid arteries
- Superior vena cava
- Ascending aorta
- Heart
- Descending aorta
- Inferior vena cava
- Femoral vein
- Femoral artery
- Capillaries

Respiratory system

The respiratory system controls your breathing.

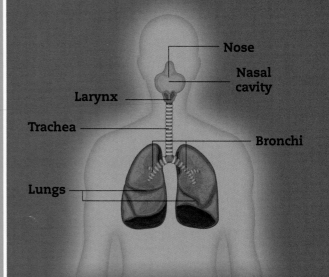

- Nose
- Nasal cavity
- Larynx
- Trachea
- Bronchi
- Lungs

This is your quick reference guide to the main systems of the body: skeletal, muscular, respiratory, circulatory, digestive, nervous, endocrine, and lymphatic.

Digestive system

The digestive system takes food in and out of your body.

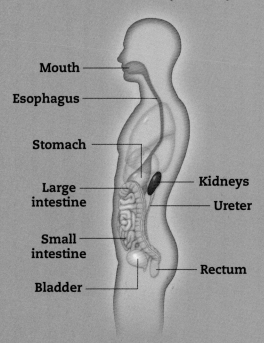

- Mouth
- Esophagus
- Stomach
- Large intestine
- Small intestine
- Bladder
- Kidneys
- Ureter
- Rectum

Nervous system

The nervous system carries messages around your body and controls everything you do.

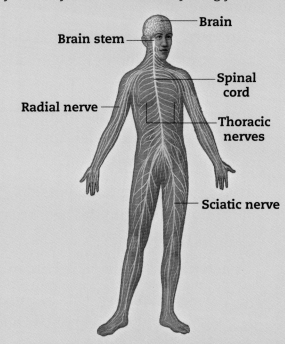

- Brain
- Brain stem
- Spinal cord
- Radial nerve
- Thoracic nerves
- Sciatic nerve

Endocrine system

The endocrine system produces hormones and controls your growth and mood.

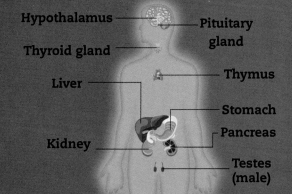

- Hypothalamus
- Pituitary gland
- Thyroid gland
- Thymus
- Liver
- Stomach
- Pancreas
- Kidney
- Testes (male)
- Ovaries (female)

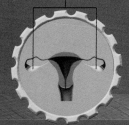

Lymphatic system

The lymphatic system fights off germs and helps keep your body healthy.

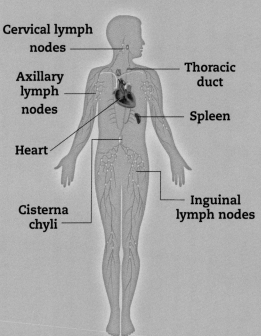

- Cervical lymph nodes
- Thoracic duct
- Axillary lymph nodes
- Spleen
- Heart
- Cisterna chyli
- Inguinal lymph nodes

GLOSSARY

abdomen The area of your body just above and below your belly button.

antibody A protein produced by the body to attack and destroy invaders such as bacteria.

antiseptic A substance that helps to stop the growth and development of harmful organisms.

artery One of the main vessels carrying blood from the heart to other parts of the body.

bacteria Tiny one-celled organisms.

capillary One of the smallest of the body's blood vessels.

diaphragm The large muscle beneath the lungs that plays a vital role in breathing.

dysentery An infection of the intestines that causes severe diarrhea.

enzyme A special protein that helps chemical reactions occur.

epinephrine (adrenaline) A hormone produced by the adrenal gland in response to stress, such as fear.

fungi Small organisms that form part of a larger group including yeasts and mushrooms.

gland An organ that regulates the release of hormones into the bloodstream.

hormone A chemical that helps to regulate processes such as reproduction and growth.

hypothalamus The area of the brain that controls the autonomic nervous system and the production of hormones by the pituitary gland.

immune system The organs and processes in the body that provide the body's defenses against infection.

intestines The large and small intestines are the part of the digestive system where nutrients are released from the food into the bloodstream.

ligament A band of strong tissue that connects the ends of bones or holds an organ in place.

liver The large organ in the abdomen that has many functions including filtering the blood before it enters the bloodstream.

lymph node One of the small lumps of tissue, particularly in the neck, armpit, and groin, where lymph is filtered.

lymphatic system A network of thin tubes, like blood vessels, that transports cells to fight infection and carries a clear liquid (lymph) to take dead cells away.

lysozyme An enzyme present in bodily fluids such as tears, saliva, and mucus that attacks invading bacteria.

malaria An infectious disease that causes fever and sweating. It is transmitted by infected mosquitoes.

marrow The soft tissue inside sections of large bone where new blood cells are produced.

mucus A slippery substance produced by the body to protect against infection.

platelet A blood cell that helps healing by binding with other platelets to form a scab.

protozoa A tiny one-celled organism that normally lives in water or soil.

red blood cell One of the blood cells that carry oxygen.

spleen Part of the lymphatic system, it produces and removes blood cells.

vein One of the main vessels carrying blood from different parts of the body to the heart.

virus A tiny organism that cannot grow or reproduce unless it is inside the cell of another organism.

white blood cell A cell that helps to fight infection in the body.

FURTHER READING

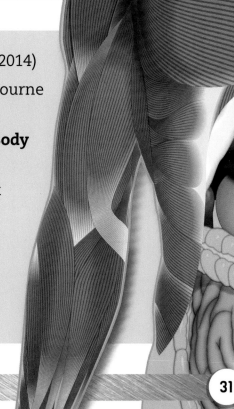

Body Works by Anna Claybourne (QED Publishing, 2014)

Complete Book of the Human Body by Anna Claybourne (Usborne Books, 2013)

Everything You Need to Know about the Human Body by Patricia MacNair (Kingfisher, 2011)

Horrible Science: Body Owner's Handbook by Nick Arnold (Scholastic Press, 2014)

Mind Webs: Human Body by Anna Claybourne (Wayland, 2014)

Project Science: Human Body by Sally Hewitt (Franklin Watts, 2012)

INDEX

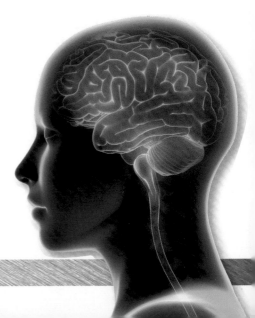